Community Workers

Helping You Heal

A Book About Nurses

Sarah C. Wohlrabe

Illustrated by Eric Thomas

T0084865

Thanks to our advisers for their expertise, research, knowledge, and advice:

Karen E. Johnson, R.N., Edina, Minnesota

Susan Kesselring, M.A., Literacy Educator
Rosemount-Apple Valley-Eagan (Minnesota) School District

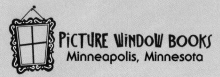

PICTURE WINDOW BOOKS
Minneapolis, Minnesota

To the best nurse ever. Thanks, Mom! —S.C.W.

Managing Editor: Bob Temple
Creative Director: Terri Foley
Editor: Peggy Henrikson
Editorial Adviser: Andrea Cascardi
Copy Editor: Laurie Kahn
Designer: John Moldstad
Page production: Picture Window Books
The illustrations in this book were prepared digitally.

Picture Window Books
1710 Roe Crest Drive
North Mankato, Minnesota 56003
www.capstonepub.com

Library of Congress Cataloging-in-Publication Data
Wohlrabe, Sarah C., 1976–
Helping you heal : a book about nurses / written by Sarah C. Wohlrabe ; illustrated by Eric Thomas.
p. cm. — (Community workers)
Summary: Describes some of the things that nurses do to help people stay healthy.
Includes bibliographical references and index.
ISBN-13: 978-1-4048-0086-1 (library binding)
ISBN-10: 1-4048-0086-7 (library binding)
ISBN-13: 978-1-4048-0480-7 (paperback)
ISBN-10: 1-4048-0480-3 (paperback)
1. Nursing—Juvenile literature. [1. Nursing. 2. Occupations.] I. Thomas, Eric, ill. II. Title.
III. Community workers (Picture Window Books)
RT61.5 .W64 2004
610.73—dc21   2003004198

Many people
in your community
have jobs helping others.

What do nurses do?

Nurses take care of you when you are sick

and teach you ways to stay healthy.

Nurses work in offices, hospitals,

and schools.

Nurses check your weight.

Nurses measure you.

How much did I grow this year?

Nurses take your temperature

and check to see how hard
your heart is working.

Nurses play funny buzzing or ringing noises in your ears.

This machine checks your hearing.

13

Nurses ask you
to cover one eye

and then the other.

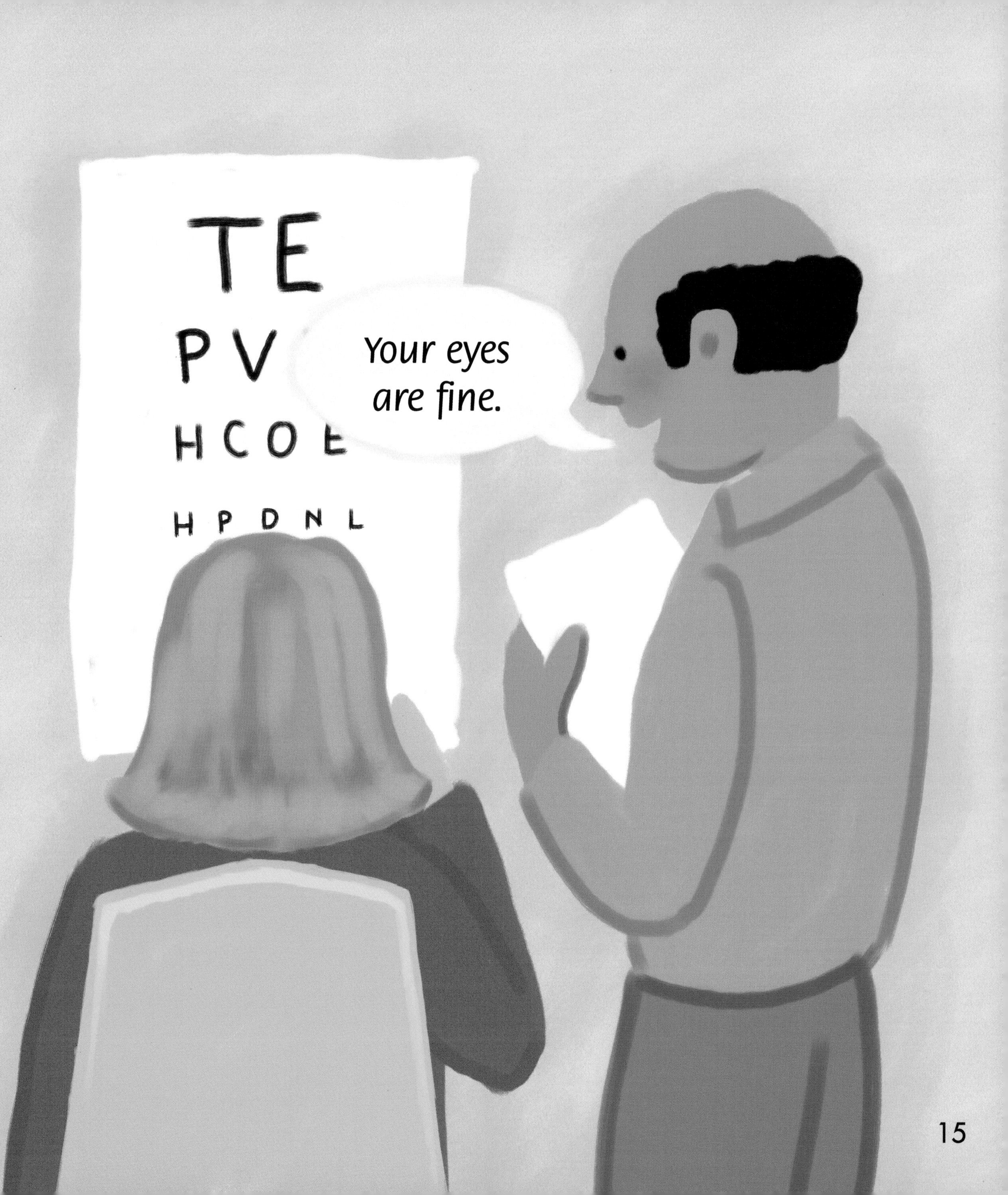
TE
PV
HPDNL
Your eyes are fine.

Sometimes nurses have to check your blood

or give you a shot of medicine.

What color bandage would you like?

Nurses wash cuts

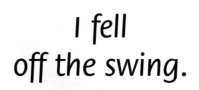

and put cold packs on bumps and bruises.

Nurses help you feel better.

Nurses help you heal.

Did You Know?

- A nurse named Florence Nightingale started nursing as we know it today. British soldiers called her the Lady with the Lamp because she walked the hospital halls all hours of the night, holding a candlelit lamp.

- In 1860, Florence Nightingale started the first school for nurses at St. Thomas's Hospital in London, England.

- Every year, Nurses Week is the week of May 12, Florence Nightingale's birthday.

- More men than ever before are going into nursing. Until the 1960s, only about 1 out of every 100 nurses was a man. By the early 2000s, more than 10 out of every 100 nursing students were men.

- Hospitals were used in India more than 2,100 years ago. The oldest hospital still in use today is in Paris, France. This hospital was started more than 1,300 years ago.

Tools for Nurses

This chart shows some of the tools nurses use for the many jobs they do.

Tool	How the Nurse Uses It
audiometer	to check hearing
blood-pressure cuff	to measure blood pressure (how hard your heart is working)
patient chart	to record patient information
stethoscope	to listen to the heart and lungs
syringe	to give shots of medicine
thermometer	to measure body temperature

Words to Know

blood pressure (BLUHD PRESH-ur)—how hard the blood is pushing against the walls of the tiny tubes in which it flows throughout the body. Blood pressure tells you how hard the heart is working.

community (kuh-MYOO-nuh-tee)—a group of people who live in the same area

cuff (KUHF)—a wide band that goes around something. The nurse puts a blood-pressure cuff around the top part of your arm and tightens it to check your blood pressure.

healthy (HEL-thee)—feeling good, without sickness or pain

hospital (HOSS-pi-tuhl)—a building where nurses, doctors, and others work to help people who are very sick or badly hurt

medicine (MED-uh-suhn)—a substance used to help sick or injured people (or animals) get better

patient (PAY-shuhnt)—someone who is being treated, or helped, by a nurse or a doctor

To Learn More

At the Library

Burby, Liza N. *A Day in the Life of a Nurse*. New York: PowerKids Press, 1999.

Flanagan, Alice K. *Ask Nurse Pfaff, She'll Help You!* New York: Children's Press, 1997.

Klingel, Cynthia Fitterer, and Robert B. Noyed. *Nurses*. Minneapolis: Compass Point Books, 2003.

Schaefer, Lola M. *We Need Nurses*. Mankato, Minn.: Pebble Books, 2000.

Vickers, Rebecca. *Florence Nightingale*. Chicago: Heinemann Library, 2000.

On the Web

Fact Hound

Fact Hound offers a safe, fun way to find Web sites related to this book. All of the sites on Fact Hound have been researched by our staff.

1. Go to *www.facthound.com*
2. Type in this special code: 1404800867
3. Click on the FETCH IT button.

Your trusty Fact Hound will fetch the best sites for you!

Index

blood pressure, 11, 23

cold packs, 19

cuts, 18

ears, 12

eyes, 14–15

hearing, 12–13, 23

hospitals, 6, 22

Nightingale, Florence, 22

nursing, 22

shots, 17, 23

temperature, 10, 23

tools for nurses, 23

weight, 8

where nurses work, 6–7